# THE
# LITTLE
# BOOK OF
# STRESS

# THE LITTLE BOOK OF
# STRESS

Rohan Candappa

**BARNES**
**& NOBLE**
**BOOKS**

NEW YORK

This edition published in 2003 exclusively for Barnes & Noble, Inc,
by Andrews McMeel Publishing.

ISBN: 0-7607-4830-6

Stress. Is it really all bad? Or is it just misunderstood?

Perhaps its only crime is to have fallen foul of a conspiracy of

namby-pamby, New Age do-gooders. Well, enough is enough.

It's time to put the record straight. Time to proclaim the most

radical philosophical truth. Time to admit that stress is good.

Because without stress we would all be very, very, very nice.

And stomach-churningly contented. And, in all honesty,

who wants to live in a world like that?

The simple teachings I have collected in this little book show you

how to increase the level of stress both within you and those

around you. It is by no means a definitive guide. But it is a start.

I hope you find it useful.

## THE REMOTE CONTROL STRATAGEM

Find out when your friends'

favorite TV program is on.

Then call them seven minutes

after it starts.

## HUSBAND YOUR RESOURCES

When you ask a woman any question,

suggest she checks with her husband

before answering.


This is even more productive if you are

a woman yourself.

EVEN IN YOUR SLEEP YOU CAN

GENERATE STRESS

Learn to snore.

## IT'S QUICKER BY TUBE

Squeeze the toothpaste tube from

the middle.

Never replace the cap.

## TAKE FIZZICAL

## EXERCISE

Whenever you have the opportunity,

shake up cans and bottles of fizzy drinks.

Then leave them for someone else to open.

## THE WAITING GAME

Always be late.

## FRIENDS

Choose friends you don't like.

## FAN THE FLAMES

Always join in other people's arguments.

Try to get others to join in, too.

## PRACTICE BUTTON PUSHING

If you have free time during the rush hour,

find a pedestrian crossing and repeatedly

push the button to stop the traffic.

Never actually cross the road.

## DON'T CHANGE

Never have the right change for anything.

# THE MILK OF
# HUMAN UNKINDNESS

Put empty milk cartons back in the fridge.

### FROM GREEN TO RED

When you're the first car in line at

a traffic light, get out and read a map.

Try to miss the green light at least twice.

## Late again

If you're enjoying a physical relationship

with a new man, give it a few weeks and then

tell him you've missed your period.


This information is best left on

an answering machine.

## Be foreign

Be German. Or whatever . . .

## ROLL WITH THE PUNCHES

If someone is telling you a joke and you know

the punch line, wait until they've nearly finished,

then tell them you've heard it before.

# THE CALMER SUTURE

Stitch people up as often as possible.

Especially your friends.

FORGET THE MOVIES—

ENJOY THE TALKIES

Go to a movie. Sit near other people.

Hold a conversation with a friend.

IN A WAY YOU'RE

SAVING THEM TIME

On the way out of the movie, if there's

a line waiting to go in, discuss the ending

in a loud voice with your friend.

SOUND ADVICE

Record the sound of a dentist's drill.

Play it at bedtime.

KNOW LIMITS

Recognize your limitations.

Then ignore them.

IT'S BETTER THAT

THEY SHOULD KNOW

Recognize other people's limitations.

Then tell people what they are.

DON'T YOU JUST HATE IT

WHEN THAT HAPPENS?

Call your friends when they're out.

Hang up just after the answering

machine starts recording.

Repeat.

## RUSH HOUR

Always travel during rush hour.

Pay your toll fee with a credit card.

# A SALE

## 1

Go to a sale on the first day when

the crowds are the biggest.

Then buy something you'll

never, ever wear.

A SALE

2

Go to a sale near the end
when it's quieter.

Beat yourself up over all the bargains
you've missed.

## SCANNER MANNERS

In the supermarket deface all the bar codes of

your items so they won't scan.

IF I DON'T DO IT...

Don't delegate. They'll only do it wrong.

ENCOURAGE COFFEE

BREAKDOWNS

Switch the decaffeinated and caffeinated

coffees around whenever you can.

DRIVE THEM MAD

Switch lanes often in your car.

Never use your turn signal.

CAN DO

Hide the can opener.

When you visit your friends' homes,

hide theirs.

COMPLICATE

The more things you must do

in life, the more things you own,

manage, or are responsible for,

the more things can go wrong.

THE BEST POLICY

Be honest.

All the time.

With everyone.

About everything.

THE BETTER POLICY

Lie.

All the time.

To everyone.

About everything.

BE RUDE

Practice rudeness,

not just to make others feel bad, but also to

make you feel bad about yourself.

It's a win-win situation.

N E V E R   F O R G I V E

Forgiving is a sign of weakness.

People will despise you for it.

NURTURING IS GOOD

Nurture your grievances.

If you don't they'll die

and then whoever's done you wrong

will have got away with it.

EVEN IN THE

SMALLEST SPACES

Fart in confined spaces.

But only if other people are present.

## CARPE DIEM

From the Latin "carpe" —to carp or whine,

and "diem" —meaning daily,

hence "carpe diem" —whine daily.

CAR PARK DIEM

When out driving, if you see

an opportunity to box someone in

by parking too close to them,

seize it.

## REJECTION

Apply for jobs you're totally unsuited for.

Keep all the rejection letters to read whenever

you start to feel good about yourself.

## DIET HARD

Eat less fresh food.

Eat more things containing preservatives.

Preservatives are called preservatives because

they help you live longer.

## LOST LOVE

Make a list of all the people

who've ever dumped you.

Contact them once a year and try

to restart the relationship.

GET LOST, LOVE

Make a list of all the people

you've ever dumped.

Contact them once a year and try

to restart the relationship.

THERE IS USE CRYING

Always buy milk in cartons you find

difficult to open.

BECOME A JUNKIE

Get a job writing junk mail.

AFTER HOURS

Always work late.

It'll make you feel tired, irritable,

and exploited.

WORKING LATE — THE

DOUBLE WHAMMY

Always work late.

Everyone else in the company

will hate you for it.

Except your boss who will despise

your gullibility.

REJOICE IN SMALL PRINT

Small print annoys everyone.

The people who read it.

The people who don't read it.

Even the people who write it.

It's great stuff.

A FROWN WILL

NEVER LET YOU DOWN

A frown communicates both

disapproval of others and unhappiness

within yourself.

IS YOUR BAR

TOO LOW?

Often it's very hard to live up

to the standards we set for ourselves.

However, sometimes we do.

To ensure this never happens, make a habit

of constantly raising the standards

you set for yourself.

# TAKE CREDIT

Take credit for successes that have

nothing to do with you.

YOU NEED THE

RIGHT BACKING

If you spend most of your day sitting at

a desk, invest in a really cheap chair.

Make sure it doesn't give your

back any support.

## TEMPERS FUGIT

Buy and wear a second watch.

Set it to beep every half hour so you can

panic about being behind schedule.

# SCHEDULES

Make them whenever possible.

Include an unrealistic number of tasks.

Agonize over why you're constantly

falling behind.

HFZ

Make yourself a Humor Free Zone.

If you ever find yourself laughing at a

predicament you're in, go to the bathroom

and pull yourself together.

PERSPECTIVE AND PROPORTION

It is no coincidence that painting

got much better when artists discovered perspective

and proportion.

So avoid both.

They are no help at all to the

dedicated disciples of stress.

# THE PRESENT TENSE

Really tense up all your muscles.

Try to stay this way all day.

If this proves impossible, you have yet again

failed at a really simple task.

IT DOES YOU CREDIT

Apply for as many credit cards as you can.

Max them out.

Then get more credit cards

and do the same.

## IMPULSE DRIVE

Never resist an impulse purchase.

Research has shown that impulse purchases

are the ones most likely to cause regret the

minute you get home. They're also the ones

most likely to encourage marital disharmony.

# CULTIVATE PST

Postshopping Stress can easily

be cultivated.

For instance, after you've bought an

expensive item, call all the stores

to discover that you could have bought it

considerably cheaper elsewhere.

## MORE HASTE

Just as you can be influenced by the group

around you, with a little determination

you can influence them. A simple technique

is to rush and nag everyone into

doing things faster than they want.

# COMMUNICATION BREAKDOWNS

If you are stressed, make sure

you communicate this to those around you.

Soon they'll be stressed too.

THE MEANING OF LIFE

Be mean. No one likes a meany.

Dedicated meanyness can really irritate

and annoy those around you. This technique

is especially recommended to

those who have, or are paid,

a lot of money.

# TURN ON, TURN UP

Turn on and turn up all the appliances in any room you are in.

Never turn anything off.

TURNIP

One day a week eat only turnips.

ALL THE FUN OF
THE UNFAIR

As a child whenever I used to wail,

"That's not fair,"

my mother used to reply,

"Life's not fair."

Why change things now?

# THE FRESH FRUIT STRATAGEM

Buy fresh fruit and put it in a bowl.

Then watch it rot.

This will make you feel bad because:

1. You're wasting money.

2. You're failing at something

   that's good for you.

# CREATE A
## DEPRESSION BANK

Stockpile memories of things that

really depress you.

Remember them, relive them,

reflect on them.

Fit them into your daily routine.

OLD FLAMES CAN

STILL BURN

Keep a photo of a past lover

somewhere your current love is

bound to find it.

# HOW TO WIN AT LOSING

## I

Buy small, expensive things
that are easy to lose.

# How to win at losing

## 2

Buy large, expensive things
and find ways of losing them.

EDEN WAS

A GARDEN

Gardening is relaxing.

Never garden.

## DON'T STOP

If you're not getting anywhere with

a task that is becoming increasingly frustrating,

don't stop. On no account walk away from it.

Research shows that the more stressed

you are the more likely you are to solve

the problem.

# THE TRUTH ABOUT

## BUSINESS

In any business encounter, always remember
that the other person is out to screw you.

# THE TRUTH ABOUT

## BOSSES

At work, never forget that any initiative

that comes from management is really a

well-disguised way of getting you to work

more for less money.

# SMUG AS A BUG

## IN A RUG

Be smug. Smug people are really annoying.

No one likes smug people.

In fact anthropologists have discovered

that in all societies, all over the world,

smug people are hated.

LEAVE LATE

When going anywhere make sure
you set off late.

Especially if you're going to an
important appointment.

# NO ONE LIKES
## A CRY BABY

Never cry. Crying is a sign of weakness.

In fact, only sissies cry.

It is far better to bottle up your

unhappiness inside you where it can grow like

a giant fungus deep within a rotting tree stump.

EXPERIENCE

THE SUNRISE

Sunrise is a deeply spiritual and uplifting time.

However, if you stay up all night

to see it you'll be so tired you'll

see it for the disappointing everyday

event it really is.

SLASH AND BURN

Plants are soothing.

They make you feel closer to nature.

Never have them in the house.

Try not to have them in the garden.

EVERY CLOUD DOESN'T

HAVE A SILVER LINING

Don't fall for this drivel. It's just deeply unscientific

propaganda put out by optimists. In fact, it's more

likely that every cloud has a lead lining

which means all our reservoirs are full

of poisoned water.

BE TOUCHY,

NOT TOUCHY-FEELY

Isolate yourself from human contact.

Shout at anyone who tries to invade your

personal space.

## A TOUCHY EXCEPTION

The only time it is permissible to touch someone is when that person has made it clear they are uncomfortable with physical contact.

PEANUTS ENVY

When entertaining guests make sure
to serve them a bowl of peanuts
as munchies, while keeping a bowl of
macadamia nuts for yourself.

## BREATHE FASTER

The faster you breathe, the more air

you get. It's a way of getting one up on

those around you. You're breathing air

that should rightfully be theirs.

And they can't do anything about it.

## DEPRESS YOURSELF EARLY

As soon as you wake up in the morning

turn on a radio news show.

News is always bad.

What better way to put you in the

right frame of mind for the day?

THE TIMES THEY

AREN'T A-CHANGING

You know the saying

"a change is as good as a rest"?

Well, it's a lie. Change invariably

makes things worse.

Resist it.

BECOME A POLITICIAN

# DON'T ONLY WORRY

## ABOUT BIG THINGS

Small things need to be worried about too.

And if you have no big things to worry about,

worry about two small things.

(The stress generated will be the same.)

GO SIP FROM THE

POISONED FOUNTAIN

Listen to gossip.

Pass it on to everybody.

And embellish it in the telling.

MAKE WAR, NOT LOVE

Try to replace lovemaking with arguing.

And if you find your arguments getting a little

routine, try spicing things up by

arguing in unusual locations.

HOME IS WHERE

THE HEARTACHE IS

Move home. Twice a year.

Every year.

MARRIAGE GUIDANCE

Get married as often as possible.

# How to turn wedding

## BELLS INTO A RIGHT

### DING-DONG

When getting married insist on
having more guests on your side
than your partner.

SWEET DREAMS

A double espresso just before bed

is always a winner.

CLEAR AIR TURBULENCE

Never "clear the air."

Instead investigate all the subtle nuances

of the word "fester."

# THEY'RE JUST NOT TRYING

When traveling abroad remember foreigners can understand English if you talk loudly and slowly.

"But I love him/her"

Constantly choose the wrong partner.

Always turn to the same friend for support

when things go wrong.

CONTEMPLATE

YOUR NOVEL

When reflecting on the many failures in

your life, remember how you've done nothing

about that novel you've always

said you were going to write.

## PETS

Research shows that people with pets live longer.

Never get a pet. And encourage your friends' and neighbors' pets to run away.

## THE LAST WORD

Always make sure you have the last word.

Raise the stakes by making that last word

"dickhead."

BORROWED DISINTEREST

Never return things you borrow.

### KEEP UP

Keep up with the Joneses.

Learn the names of everyone on your street.

Keep up with them too.

NO SMOKE WITHOUT IRE

1. Smoke.

2. Smoke cigars.

3. Smoke cigars in "No Smoking" areas.

USEFUL PHRASE

"Why did you do that?"

## SHOPPING

Do your weekly shopping in a big
supermarket on a Saturday morning.
Take your children with you.
If you don't have any children
of your own, borrow some.

WHAT FRIENDS

ARE FOR

Always borrow money from friends.

Forget or put off repaying it for as long

as possible.

S I N G L E D   O U T

Ask single women if they've got

a boyfriend yet.

Repeat on Valentine's Day.

IT'S GOOD TO TALK

At dinner parties try to bring the

conversation around to sex, religion,

or politics.

Preferably all three.

COUNT YOUR BLESSINGS

Why?

You haven't got any.

Count your problems instead.

## ROUTINES

Routines are good.

Have routines and stick to them religiously.

Refuse to change them for any reason,

no matter how reasonable.

BECAUSE THEY CAN'T CLOSE THEIR

EARS

Cultivate an annoying voice.

## CREATE A MEMOTOCRACY

If you work in an office, get into the habit

of communicating exclusively by memo.

No one likes sleeping

IN A DAMP BED

Be a wet blanket.

CAPTAIN HOOK,
I PRESUME?

Never let yourself, or anyone else,

off the hook.

# KNOW YOUR PLACE

## I

Always remember that, in truth, you are
only a small, unimportant cog in a
massive machine you can't control.

# KNOW YOUR PLACE

2

Always remember that you are, in truth,

the center of the universe,

the very sun that everything and everyone

else should revolve around.

IS ANYONE IN CHARGE?

Deal with bureaucracies as

often as you can.

Bureaucracies are the foundation

of stress creation.

THINK ABOUT IT

Why meditate when you can worry?

Worrying is meditation carried out

by realists.

LAUGHTER—THE

WORST MEDICINE

The only time it is permissible to

laugh is when you encounter

the misfortune of others.

But you can only laugh in their presence.

BECOME A JUNK HUNK

Junk food will help you lead a rubbish life.

Eat it as often as you can.

BEDTIME READING

Write down your worries.

Read the list before you go to bed.

THE EARLY BIRD

Take offense early.

It saves time.

ADVICE ADDS SPICE

Take every opportunity to give others advice.

Especially on subjects of which you have

very little or no knowledge.

T H E   T R U T H

Recognize that true happiness depends

solely on how many material possessions

you own.

Act accordingly.

## ADD ADDITIVES

Try to maximize your additive consumption during the day.